A Blinded Horse
Dreams of Hippocampi
&
Other Plays

by
Justin Maxwell

ALLIGATOR
PEAR
PUBLISHING

Copyright © 2016 by Justin Maxwell
ALL RIGHTS RESERVED
Cover Art Design Copyright © 2016 by Chris Marroy
Editing, Layout, and Typography by Robin Baudier

CAUTION: Professionals and amateurs are hereby warned that *A Blinded Horse Dreams of Hippocampi & Other Plays* is subject to a licensing fee. It is fully protected under the copyright laws of the United States of America, The British Commonwealth, including Canada, and all other countries of the Copyright Union. All rights, including professional, amateur, motion picture, recitation, lecturing, public reading, radio broadcasting, television and the rights of translation into foreign languages are strictly reserved.

The amateur and professional live stage performance rights to *A Blinded Horse Dreams of Hippocampi & Other Plays* are controlled exclusively by Alligator Pear Publishing, LLC, and licensing arrangements and performance licenses must be secured well in advance of presentation. When applying for a licensing quotation and a performance license, be prepared to supply the number of performances intended, dates of production, seating capacity, and admission fee. Licensing fees are payable one week before the opening performance of the play to Alligator Pear Publishing, LLC. Licensing of the required amount must be paid whether the play is presented for charity or gain and whether or not admission is charged. Discounted copies of the play will be made available to licensed producers for use in their production. Permission and terms must be secured in writing from Alligator Pear Publishing, LLC, for all professional and amateur readings. Publication of this play does not imply availability for performance.

Copying from this book in whole or in part is strictly forbidden by the law, and the right of performance is not transferable. Whenever the play is produced the following notice must appear on all programs for the play: "Produced by special arrangement with Alligator Pear Publishing, LLC." Due authorship credit must be given on all programs, printing, and advertising for the play. The name of the author must appear on a separate line on which no other name appears, immediately following the title. It is not permissible to make changes to this play for the purpose of production without the written consent of the author.

For more information about the licensing described above or to contact the author for all other rights, visit www.alligatorpearpublishing.com.

for
Susan Maxwell,
thank you.

Table of Contents

Foreword i

A Blinded Horse Dreams of Hippocampi 1

Inspiration Point... 13

I'm in Al-Qaeda: a comedy of manners 29

Whatsleeves 43

~6x³=SAFETY: a comedic list poem 47

My Rich Temple.. 59

Old MacDonald Dirge... 75

Patience on the Way to Daylight: an *Ars Poetica* farce 81

Exhausted Paint: the Death of Van Gogh................................. 89

Acknowledgments 137

Foreword

by Caridad Svich

Some words here begin we begin.

This is a foreword, which means there are these words before the other words come, the words written by the author, in this case, the words of Justin Maxwell. But of course, let's not say that they are his words, but rather words in English that he has carefully arranged into his own personal theatrical syntax. Call it the language of dreams. Call it work in the realm of the impossible. Call it opera-theatre. Call it surrealist poetry. Or just say that the nine plays which you are about to experience are simply plays, which means they are events in space and events on the page.

Maxwell writes about loneliness in these short, varied, elusive, mysterious plays. He references Nick Cave, David Lynch, William Burroughs and Wittgenstein, among others. He wears his traces lightly but he wants you to know where he stands—firmly in the land of chaos, disorder, Dionysus and the unruly bacchanal, rather than in the land of Apollonian reason.

Even in the dark comedy of manners "I'm in Al-Qaeda," the subject is not necessarily entirely fear and the spectre of terrorism, but rather the alienation felt by both subjects—the Middle Eastern man and the middle class US-born woman—on the leg of an uncomfortable airplane flight.

The loneliness of which Maxwell writes is of objects and animals and humans cast adrift by contemporary and ancient society (in the case of the play "My Rich Tem ple"). Here we are in the land of remnants and scraps, old arcane songs and forgotten lullabies, sea stories and old jokes. We are in the dustbin of history, where even Vincent Van Gogh can't fight against the exhausted world in which he lives and dreams. In fact, fatigue—or shall we say, the point past where we think we can endure—is a recurring motif in these plays, which illustrate, among others, a contentious pop culture colliding love affair between an ice cream store and a car, and a blinded horse and the nightmare that consumes and/or liberates him.

In performance, and especially in certain kinds of ritualized performance works and live art pieces that explore the limits of form and the limits too of the body, there is another space where theatre sometimes lives. And here I use the words "theater" and "performance" synonymously. This space that exists past endurance, past knowledge, past all things is one sometimes of drunkenness, of liberation and/or of recognition.

How does one know oneself? By looking past and through the known mirror.

Maxwell, in these nine short plays, speeds things up and slows them down (most notably in the "Old Macdonald Dirge") past the point of familiarity. Tricked-out and tripped-out, the melancholy fervor of Maxwell's works for theatre exemplify a kind of tattered walk through variegated modes of ecstasy: bliss, joy, rage, delirium, mania and even a kind of serenity. His plays conjure worlds of fantasy, terror, and absolute defiance. The ecstatic drive coursing through these plays is nothing if not resistant to trend, consumerist theatrical maneuvers, and plain ol' logic.

Foreword

But of course there is a logic at work here. One of deliberate disruption. Fully in line with the kind of surreal dares of the puppet plays and experiments in sound, light, image and poetry of early career Federico Garcia Lorca and the legacy too of the Padua Hills Playwrights movement of the 1980s and 1990s. There, not only masters like Maria Irene Fornes wrote some of their major works but also Sam Shepard and John Steppling carved out new ways of being and seeing theatre through poetic language and action(s). There is also a firm stylistic wink and a nod in Maxwell's plays to the landscape-inflected "language" plays of Mac Wellman, Len Jenkin, Erik Ehn and early-career Suzan Lori Parks—writers that, like their counterparts on the West Coast, were seeking a different way of approaching stage words and pictures in performance spaces in once artist-affordable downtown New York City and Brooklyn.

Perhaps it could be said that Maxwell's writing is partly nostalgic for a time in US theatrical arts and letters when precisely these kinds of linguistic and imagistic experiments anchored by and rooted in text were the vanguard of the avant-garde before the tide of neoliberal ideologies in socio-politics and the turn toward global capitalism changed and upended certain value systems in the US, of which the field of theatre is not exempt.

Looking at the playful wit of "Whatsleeves" and the desperate fury of "Exhausted Paint: the death of Van Gogh" at nearly opposite ends of this volume's spectrum is to see a writer charting his own topography of joy and disgust against systems that seek to brand and codify art for commercial purposes.

What use art? Perhaps one that has not yet been divined.

Caridad Svich

If you walk along the bruised, pleasure-and-pain-filled streets of New Orleans, where this collection is being born in print, then you are walking through a whole lotta dustbins where history done laid its signs and is still looking for mighty spiritual recompense. In an age of economic austerity, where the divide between those who have much and those who have little grows exponentially, and where climate change is a fact that seems to hover conveniently out of sight from where much US governmental policy places its priorities, you could say that Maxwell's nine plays are also a lonesome cry from a rich, vast and purposefully individualistic yet plurally-minded wilderness of theatrical possibility, rather than "impossibility."

The raging fantastical beauty and terror evoked in these plays are not just coming from a place of whimsy, literary allegiance and homage to past poets and rebel rousers but also from an inescapable sense of despair at broken systems of inequity and the disavowal of the easily dispossessed in these United States.

Look under the lines of evolution that Maxwell charts and you will see from horse to seahorse to ice cream store to singer to artist a through line of dreamers that have been told dreaming is not worth doing in a land of seeming plenty. Yet Maxwell insists that dreaming is necessary, especially the kind that courts the dangerous sublime.

Risk order to create new order. Make a garden where there is blight.

Make a feast.

Of poor theatre

Rich in its love of what makes us: the irrational, the

Foreword

sacred and profane, the blessed and sometimes, too, the merely elementally silly, for it too deserves a place.

While I was reading these nine plays, I travelled to many different places in mind. I thought of old theatres with faded marquees, of garage theatres with sofas for chairs, of sidewalk interventions with ghosts of the past singing old-new songs to anyone who'd care and dare to listen. I thought of how horses can dream, and ice cream stores can speak and how someone can be one and also five selves. I thought about the smell of salt and greasy food and honky-tonks and blues bars, and of how a city looks after a late night crawl in the morning light: hungover but resilient, willing to give another day another try. I thought too of rock n' roll karma and the dharma bums of the Beats and Greil Marcus looking out for the inside of the inside of the sleeve in this ol' American record we call song.

Greil Marcus would love these plays, and I think you will too, even if you find them startling, disruptive and yes, impossible. They teach us to dream again. And that's as wondrous strange as any new world-theatre should be.

Caridad Svich received a 2012 OBIE for Lifetime Achievement, a 2013 National Latino Playwriting Award, 2012 Edgerton Foundation New Play Award and 2011 American Theatre Critics Association Primus Prize. Among her key plays are Alchemy of Desire/Dead-Man's Blues, 12 Ophelias, Iphigenia Crash Land Falls on the Neon Shell That Was Once Her Heart, The Way of Water *and* The House of the Spirits *(based on Isabel Allende's novel). She also sustains parallel careers*

Caridad Svich

as a translator, arts journalist and editor. She has edited several books on theatre including Innovation in Five Acts *(TCG, 2015) and* Out of Silence: Censorship in Theatre *(Eyecorner Press, 2014). Three of her plays are collected in the new volume* JARMAN (all this maddening beauty) and other plays *(Intellect, UK, 2016). Visit her at www.caridadsvich.com and www.nopassport.org.*

A Blinded Horse Dreams of Hippocampi

Justin Maxwell

I believe in God.
I believe in mermaids too.
I believe in 72 virgins on a chain.
Why not? Why not?
    —Nick Cave, "Mermaids"

Justin Maxwell

Characters

THE HORSE: a horse blinded by a stablehand.

THE CHORUS OF SEAHORSES: 60,000 seahorses, played by anywhere between one and 60,000 actors.

THE NIGHTMARE: Is it a horse with flaming hooves, a man with a spike, a wolf in wolf's clothing?

Time

The dreamtime.

Setting

The steppes of a horse's dreamscape.

First presented at the Mid-America Theatre Conference, 2014. First published in the journal Eleven Eleven, *issue 19, 2015.*

A Blinded Horse Dreams of Hippocampi

*Nighttime. The stars come out. We are on the vast steppes that all horses dream of. Enter **THE HORSE**, blind even here. While **THE HORSE** is speaking, **THE NIGHTMARE** enters surreptitiously.*

THE HORSE

Most nights, I can smell the ocean.
The breeze rolls the grass in trochaic breakers,
stress
        lull,
stress
        lull,
stress
        lull,
grain as surf, pollen as flotsam.
The stars sing to the navigators;
the mermaids sing to the sailors;
the seahorses sing to me,
but I am afraid of the hippocampi and their song.
I am afraid of the blurry motion of the world,
of rolling, of closing in,
of the scent of grain breezing over the steppes,
    *(realizes **THE NIGHTMARE** has arrived)*
of the Nightmare, a black horse trimmed in fire.

THE NIGHTMARE

There are things in this world to fear:
the coyote,
the rattlesnake,
the wolf,
the metal spike,
the sudden motion,
the aching void.
Me.

Justin Maxwell

THE HORSE

We do not speak to one another.
The spheres have their music;
we can attempt to listen or we can attempt to ignore.
Any answer would be impotent;
this is no place for dialog.

Better to let the waves wash over me,
pull me down among the hippocampi,
and swim.

Water is the ally of rust;
both are blunting forces.

> ***(THE CHORUS OF SEAHORSES** enters; **THE NIGHTMARE** is unhappy about their contrapuntal motion.)*

THE HORSE *(Cont'd)*

I forgive the spike
I forgive the iron hand,
but I want both to rust away.
I want to be unafraid.

THE CHORUS OF SEAHORSES

Come and see.
Come and see.
(beat)
The susurrus of the sea is its own song,
our song.
Waves make their own cadence:
wave
       trough
wave
       trough
WAVE.

A Blinded Horse Dreams of Hippocampi

Three trochaic feet make a line of the ocean's endless
epic.
A horse's heart beats a different tattoo;
the sea does not have a mammalian cadence.
Once there was a constellation named Hippocampus;
its stars helped navigators,
and some still hear our songs.
Come and see.
Come and see.

THE HORSE

There are stars at the bottom of the ocean,
a new way to navigate,
the seahorse,
the hippocampus,
curls deep inside the brain—
in it hums our songs of memory,
      orientation,
           trauma.
The hippocampus atrophies with stress,
but still grows new neurons
throughout our lives—
we can always learn trauma.
The seahorse of the ancient Greeks,
is old like starlight:
      Hippos—horse
      Kampos—sea monster.
It sings a tempting song.
It is inescapable,
      submerged in the core of our liquid-electric
      brains.
A child follows a lullaby into sleep;
a sailor follows the siren to rest on their rocks.
There is no fire underwater

Justin Maxwell

>just stars
>>and song.

Horses are creatures that follow.

THE NIGHTMARE

Then follow me.
We no longer navigate by the stars:
Bearing dial and a bag of ravens,
chart and sextant,
compass and stopwatch,
radar,
global positioning system.
Eye and light, then
darkness and song.
Always a new way to navigate.
The hippocampus is just part of the brain.
It tells you things too simple to be lies:
I am here;
I was there;
I went from here to there;
I am standing;
I am sitting;
I am prone;
I am wounded;
>I am aching
>>It is here
>>>It is there.

THE HORSE

It is deep in my brain and I
>may know the way
>>to, from, away.

To navigate is to follow;
singers sing their songs, and I

A Blinded Horse Dreams of Hippocampi

follow along.
    (beat)
Or, we follow.
Or, you follow.

THE NIGHTMARE

Only the somnambulist walks into the sea;
do not mistake "dream" for "drown."
There's no devil here,
no god,
no Homer,
no one of deep faith
nor iambic pentameter.

THE HORSE

The vast steppes,
the fathoms of the sea,
the void of space,
are all quiet cradles.
The nightmare descends and becomes
a terrestrial phenomenon.
Perhaps the rocks themselves call
to the sailors,
with sea foam for sirens.
They are justification by sensuality.

Fiery hoof prints scar the sky and evaporate.
The ship's keel groans, cracks, and shatters.
It makes a ship-shaped hole in the surface
of the sea, then it's gone.
All options are disintegration,
and even the good dreams dissipate.
So it is easy to follow,
to listen to the electric song of hippocampi.

Justin Maxwell

THE CHORUS OF SEAHORSES

Come and see
Come and see
Our song is simple.
Our song is succor.
We are the soporific dream of peace.
We are the deep, cool brine.
Come and see.
Come and see.

THE HORSE

Only after I went blind could I hear the hippocampi
call to me.
In the inscrutable stillness
their song comes across the void,
their scree appears, glowing
golden, motes on my useless eyes.
    (beat)
The breeze.
The grain shivers.
My withers tense,
motion in my darkness,
the screen of blindness,
the songs calling me down
into the depth of the sea.

THE CHORUS OF SEAHORSES

Come and see.
Come and see.
    (beat)
Evolution has brought you nothing;
return to the sea.
Brine cleanses,
salt burns away cruelty,

A Blinded Horse Dreams of Hippocampi

gives scars bioluminescence.
The sea purifies:
liquefies glaciers,
cools magma to archipelagos,
reduces stone to sand,
cliff to beach,
vents energy into the bottom of the ocean,
building fresh worlds in the blind abyss.
Come and see.
Come and see.
> *(beat)*

Immersion is our future and our past.
Become a glowing star
in our wine-dark sky.
Come and see.
Come and see.

THE HORSE
Better a singer than the song.
Better the unknown cruelty.
Better the aloof fathoms.
Better the indifferent sea.

THE NIGHTMARE
> *(resentful)*

The desiccating sun rises.
The deluging rain descends.
Bacteria grows on the grain.
Mold spores drift on the wind.
There's anthrax in the soil
and tetanus in the rust.
These are the things you know.
Stay with us.

Justin Maxwell

THE HORSE

The spike is in the hand,
the arcing sky,
the clean iron in my eyes
the rusty taste in my mouth.

I too am a singer.

Perhaps you have followed me here?
Perhaps you have heard a song?
Perhaps all songs are the same.
Perhaps I've been a seahorse all along.

Dark. End of play.

Inspiration Point

Justin Maxwell

Love is a bird of flames.
—David Lynch, "Bird of Flames"

Justin Maxwell

Characters

(both really good-looking)

ICE CREAM STORE: an ice cream store. It is resentful.

CHERRY-RED TOP-DOWN MUSCLE CAR: a car. It has transgressed.

Setting

Dunes near the ocean.

Notes

If the play is cast in a heteronormative idiom, then the **STORE** is male and the **CAR** is female.

Much of this script's energy comes from how the words and the tone contrast, thus all the parenthetical directions. The parenthetical questions are questions that audience members should have when they hear that line delivered.

The characters finish each other's thoughts in the casual way of a long-established couple. The humor is a veneer on the anger; the anger is a veneer on the sadness.

First presented at the Mid-America Theatre Conference, 2015.

Inspiration Point

Inspiration Point, some dunes near the ocean. Night. They appear exuberant.

CHERRY-RED TOP-DOWN MUSCLE CAR
I'm a cherry-red, top-down muscle car.

ICE CREAM STORE
I'm an ice cream store.

BOTH
We're in love.

CHERRY-RED TOP-DOWN MUSCLE CAR
Out there's the ocean,

ICE CREAM STORE
and a Nazi submarine.

CHERRY-RED TOP-DOWN MUSCLE CAR
The submarine is in love too.

ICE CREAM STORE
It loves the tramp steamer that's hauling war goods from New Jersey to Hampton Roads.

CHERRY-RED TOP-DOWN MUSCLE CAR
(Is there some anxiety?)
It's not the submarine's fault.

ICE CREAM STORE
The steamer has the best sonar report the sub has ever seen.

CHERRY-RED TOP-DOWN MUSCLE CAR
Mixed marriages are . . .

ICE CREAM STORE
difficult.

CHERRY-RED TOP-DOWN MUSCLE CAR
(lying)
But not for us.

BOTH
We're in love.

CHERRY-RED TOP-DOWN MUSCLE CAR
We get off work at Coney Island,

ICE CREAM STORE
go on a double date with the malt shop and a bumper car.

CHERRY-RED TOP-DOWN MUSCLE CAR
After the double date, we—

ICE CREAM STORE
just the two of us—

CHERRY-RED TOP-DOWN MUSCLE CAR
we sit out in the sand dunes and watch the waves roll in.

ICE CREAM STORE
Watch the freighter and the submarine flirt.

CHERRY-RED TOP-DOWN MUSCLE CAR
They have a difficult relationship.

ICE CREAM STORE
(Is that resentment?)
It's the way of the world, apparently.

CHERRY-RED TOP-DOWN MUSCLE CAR
They're both so buoyant. You'd think they'd find fulfillment in each other.

ICE CREAM STORE
You'd think.

CHERRY-RED TOP-DOWN MUSCLE CAR
Life's good,

ICE CREAM STORE
but sometimes

CHERRY-RED TOP-DOWN MUSCLE CAR
there are problems,

ICE CREAM STORE
which must be resolved,

CHERRY-RED TOP-DOWN MUSCLE CAR
navigated.

ICE CREAM STORE
Sometimes things are too much Nazi and not enough freighter,

CHERRY-RED TOP-DOWN MUSCLE CAR
then it's time to mix things up.
(Was that anxiety again, or maybe hope?)
Spontaneity can help one come out of their shell. It can lead to honesty, to openness.

ICE CREAM STORE
To revelation, which is . . .

CHERRY-RED TOP-DOWN MUSCLE CAR
Good.
    (beat)
There's nothing wrong with novelty.

ICE CREAM STORE
Consensual novelty.

CHERRY-RED TOP-DOWN MUSCLE CAR
It's healthy.

ICE CREAM STORE
    (A veiled threat?)
Suddenly . . .

CHERRY-RED TOP-DOWN MUSCLE CAR
I'm a 1978 AMC Pacer.

ICE CREAM STORE
And I'm Jimmy Carter.

BOTH
We're in love.

ICE CREAM STORE
It was weird to get a gender.

> *An erotically charged confession; this public exposure is an ugly-but-consensual part of their sexuality.*

Inspiration Point

CHERRY-RED TOP-DOWN MUSCLE CAR
Suddenly, I'm a ring-tailed lemur named Bosco.

ICE CREAM STORE
And I'm Betty Boop.

BOTH
We're in love.

CHERRY-RED TOP-DOWN MUSCLE CAR
It was strange to be an animal instead of a product line.

ICE CREAM STORE
Weird is the price you pay for novelty.

CHERRY-RED TOP-DOWN MUSCLE CAR
All our lint rollers were crusted in lemur leavings and glitter.

ICE CREAM STORE
(playing along)
Our mascara budget was higher than our rent.

CHERRY-RED TOP-DOWN MUSCLE CAR
Novelty helps us connect

ICE CREAM STORE
to each other

CHERRY-RED TOP-DOWN MUSCLE CAR
and to ourselves.

ICE CREAM STORE
Other times,

Justin Maxwell

CHERRY-RED TOP-DOWN MUSCLE CAR
I'm Vermeer's Girl with a Pearl Earring.

ICE CREAM STORE
And I'm Ike Turner.

BOTH
(less ebullience)
We're in love.

ICE CREAM STORE
Which, it turns out, isn't enough.

CHERRY-RED TOP-DOWN MUSCLE CAR
And being made in America

ICE CREAM STORE
means we aren't very imaginative.

CHERRY-RED TOP-DOWN MUSCLE CAR
Popular,

ICE CREAM STORE
but not imaginative.

CHERRY-RED TOP-DOWN MUSCLE CAR
It's hard to learn how to feel,

ICE CREAM STORE
instead of just feeling more.

CHERRY-RED TOP-DOWN MUSCLE CAR
But we try.

Inspiration Point

ICE CREAM STORE
Suddenly,

CHERRY-RED TOP-DOWN MUSCLE CAR
I'm Tony Kushner.

ICE CREAM STORE
And I'm Tony Kushner.

BOTH
We're in love.

ICE CREAM STORE
And we talk about it,

CHERRY-RED TOP-DOWN MUSCLE CAR
a lot.

ICE CREAM STORE
That one wasn't fun.

CHERRY-RED TOP-DOWN MUSCLE CAR
I got TMJ.

ICE CREAM STORE
We weren't getting good results.

CHERRY-RED TOP-DOWN MUSCLE CAR
But we kept trying,

ICE CREAM STORE
exploring.

Justin Maxwell

CHERRY-RED TOP-DOWN MUSCLE CAR
We didn't have gender before,

ICE CREAM STORE
just cultural associations,

CHERRY-RED TOP-DOWN MUSCLE CAR
and subtext.

ICE CREAM STORE
Suddenly,

CHERRY-RED TOP-DOWN MUSCLE CAR
(not happy)
I'm a Caananite temple prostitute named Jolene,

ICE CREAM STORE
and I'm the Mormon Tabernacle Choir.

BOTH
We're in love.

CHERRY-RED TOP-DOWN MUSCLE CAR
A "theme night" taught us

ICE CREAM STORE
(Hurt?)
that we needed ground rules.

CHERRY-RED TOP-DOWN MUSCLE CAR
(An apology, or just sadness?)
But rules can feel oppressive.

ICE CREAM STORE
(Also hurt?)
I just wanted us both to be happy all the time.

CHERRY-RED TOP-DOWN MUSCLE CAR
Attention can feel like love too.

ICE CREAM STORE
(malicious)
Now we know better than that, don't we.

CHERRY-RED TOP-DOWN MUSCLE CAR
(remorseful)
We're supposed to.

ICE CREAM STORE
And yet,

CHERRY-RED TOP-DOWN MUSCLE CAR
(down)
I was Helen.

ICE CREAM STORE
(also down)
And I was the population of Troy.

BOTH
We were in love.

ICE CREAM STORE
I never thought I'd need to learn about "safe words."

CHERRY-RED TOP-DOWN MUSCLE CAR
(Faking happiness?)
Our safe word is: "Agamemnon."

Justin Maxwell

ICE CREAM STORE
Because it's hard to forget,

CHERRY-RED TOP-DOWN MUSCLE CAR
and it can be easily understood—
>*(beat)*

even when your voice is muffled like a submarine.

ICE CREAM STORE
>*(stern)*

Also . . .

CHERRY-RED TOP-DOWN MUSCLE CAR
That's all.

ICE CREAM STORE
>*(threat)*

Also.

CHERRY-RED TOP-DOWN MUSCLE CAR
I'm ashamed.

ICE CREAM STORE
Good.
>*(beat)*

Also.

CHERRY-RED TOP-DOWN MUSCLE CAR
I was Jim Henson.

ICE CREAM STORE
And I was Miss Piggy.

Inspiration Point

BOTH
(one swearing, one sad)
We were in love.

CHERRY-RED TOP-DOWN MUSCLE CAR
(sincere)
But love is

ICE CREAM STORE
a sonar ping in the void,

CHERRY-RED TOP-DOWN MUSCLE CAR
and we couldn't imagine better sounds.

ICE CREAM STORE
We didn't know how to play with bliss.

CHERRY-RED TOP-DOWN MUSCLE CAR
Because I'm a car.

ICE CREAM STORE
And I'm a small business.

CHERRY-RED TOP-DOWN MUSCLE CAR
(sad)
I don't know why watching the waves can't sustain us.

Dark. The first strains of David Lynch's "Football Game" are heard. End of play.

Justin Maxwell

I'm in Al-Qaeda

a comedy of manners

Justin Maxwell

Characters

MAN: Afghani/Pakistani, very serious. Nearly dead. Late 30s. Dressed in an offensively stereotypical fashion, maybe even with a towel for a turban. But he only has the slightest of accents. At this point in his life he hates talking, but it is cathartic. And his only survival mechanism.

WOMAN: An extrovert and a bit of a worrier, early 30s. Newly upper middle class and proud of it—very middle America, very small town. She's way overdressed for a plane trip.

Setting

We are in the first class cabin of a commercial airliner, probably just represented by two chairs.

Time

Late in the second Bush administration.

First produced at The Brick Theater's Democracy Festival in New York City, June 2012.

I'm in Al-Qaeda

*Two first class plane seats in spotlight. In one sits a seriously angry-looking **MAN**; he has a thick beard and looks ill.*

*The **WOMAN** enters, looking for her seat. This is her first time in First Class, and she's all abuzz with WASP-y comeuppance. Then she realizes which seat is hers. She sits down, hoping he's an oil tycoon or something, and tries to make the best of it.*

WOMAN
(nervous but upbeat)
I'm on my way to Tulsa, to see my sister.

MAN
(flat)
I'm in Al-Qaeda.

WOMAN
(nervous laughter, then real laughter)
That's so not funny!
I don't think President Bush would find that funny.

MAN
I apologize if my tone communicated humor.

WOMAN
Oh. Well, that didn't seem like the kind of thing one would just . . . say.

MAN
Oh.

WOMAN
(still trying to make a joke)
How did you get through security?

MAN

No metal.

WOMAN

?

MAN

No liquids.

WOMAN

How can you say these things?
What if I was an air marshal?

We hear the sound of the plane taking off.

WOMAN *(Cont'd)*
Tell me the truth, or I'll call the stewardess.

MAN

Gretchen made peace with this months ago.
    (beat)
So does this mean you're not the CIA interrogator?

WOMAN
(still trying to joke)
Then wouldn't we be in some dingy back room with a drain in the floor?

MAN
(taking off the disgusting towel/turban)
When they asked me questions, I told them everything

I knew.
When they beat me, I told them about my goats.
When they electrocuted me, I said everything I knew about Angora goats. They're really the best, by the way.
I was depressed that the mock execution wasn't real, so I just made up stuff about guys named "Abdul."
I tried to drown myself in the water boarding bucket and then made up weird stories about the Nation of Islam. But they didn't believe a goat herder would know about that.
I attempted to convert to Christianity.
Now they're doing this.

WOMAN
What?

MAN
Air travel. They force me to fly from city to city. I get off one plane, check in on another flight and get on the next plane. It's hell. I stand in security lines and sit on tarmacs, and get air sick, and I don't really sleep, and the toilets in Detroit are too filthy to drown myself in. / And

WOMAN
(sudden trepidation)
My layover is in Detroit!
This plane is going to stop there.
I mean Detroit. It just has such a reputation. You know?

MAN
Not really.
(beat)
The first time I saw a dinosaur was in the Detroit airport.

WOMAN
?

MAN
They have a real, fossilized brontosaurus over the security checkpoint. My homeland doesn't even have a museum.

WOMAN
(nervously trying to joke)
All that way. You must get the best frequent flyer deals.

MAN
(pleasurelessly)
I have 48 A Plus Rewards Points on Airtran.
I have 3,523 Flight Fund, Fund Bucks on American West—the CIA just keeps sending me to Phoenix.
I have 12,220 AAdvantage Miles with American
32,000 Skymiles with Delta
1,870 Midwest Miles on Midwest Airlines
I have 26,000 World Perks Miles on Northwest. If they merge with Delta, I'll get a free ticket to Lahore, and I might be able to escape all this.
I have 8,000 Dividend Miles on US Airways.
My Mileage Plus Plan with United is out of this world, but not out of the contiguous 48.
(beat)
The happiest moment of my current life was when I saw the Pakistan/Guam World Cup match in the Delta Crown Room Club in Chicago. I had some tea and took a nap.

WOMAN
I can't imagine the government would spend taxpayer money like that.

MAN

Oh, I'm an air marshal.

WOMAN

?

MAN

The government lists me as an off-duty air marshal. So I still have to go through security, but they don't have to buy a seat. I just have all the rigmarole.

WOMAN

So you could have a gun?

MAN

I'M a GOAT HERDER. The most violent thing I do is sheer.

WOMAN

You're really not funny anymore. If you were a detainee, wouldn't you be in a jumpsuit or something?

MAN

When I was picked up in the Gomal Valley, I was wearing off-brand jeans, flip-flops, and a Buffalo Bills Super Bowl Champions 1992 T-shirt. I hate the Buffalo Airport so much. One concourse, 26 gates, and the coke machine doesn't give out change.

WOMAN

Well, not all of America is Buffalo, you know. Some parts are just lovely.

MAN
I only see it through eleven by seven Plexiglas windows.

WOMAN
My sister's husband Harvey has the largest collection of porcelain cowboys in Texarkana.

MAN
(ignoring her)
As far as I can tell, this whole country reeks of formaldehyde.

WOMAN
Don't be ridiculous.

MAN
Drips with it.

WOMAN
Why would you say that?

MAN
Because in about forty minutes we'll be coated in formaldehyde.

WOMAN scowls in uncomprehending disapproval.

MAN *(Cont'd)*
Really. I mean . . . literally. Domestic flights don't contain oxygen scrubbers. So while you're on a plane the levels of ozone and carbon monoxide build up in the cabin. When they come into contact with the oils that skin naturally produces they form chemicals called

I'm in Al-Qaeda

nonanal and decanal. These become formaldehyde, very toxic, probably carcinogenic.

WOMAN
(indignant)
Maybe in wherever you're from. But here there are Unions to protect workers. And OSHA. And consumer advocacy groups to advocate for the consumer. You're really not funny you know.

MAN
Oh, and there's a neurotoxin called tricresyl phosphate that slowly builds up in the cabin. Oh, and a 25 % reduction in oxygen levels while in the air. Oh, and vaporized oil and hydraulic fluid from the engines, both of which are crazy poisonous.

WOMAN
Well, then how do the pilots even survive?

MAN
They get ten times more oxygen pumped to them than the rest of us.

WOMAN
How can you know all this?

MAN
Three hours on a broken plane, at the gate, between Continental's Pilots' Union Rep and their Flight Attendants' Rep, at Logan International.
Six hours next to a medical student specializing in poison control on the tarmac at O'Hare.
Five hour layover in Denver gave me time to double

check with a chemist who works at Dow.
Two hours in a holding pattern over Ronald Regan with a drunken formaldehyde salesman.
(beat)
Maybe Allah wants me to understand irony.

WOMAN

I doubt it.

MAN

Oh, and I sat next to a House member last week who missed his connection in Miami-Dade and is on a committee to do something about doing something about this.

WOMAN

Probably some democrat.

MAN

(thinks for a moment)
I always wanted the big government tribal warlords to leave me alone and let me herd goats in peace.

WOMAN

So you're a right-wing, Pashtun goat herder?
(trying to joke again)
I thought you were in Al-Qaeda.

MAN

Do I look Pashtun?
(beat)
I wasn't in Al-Qaeda when I was kidnapped and sold to the CIA.
I wonder who's got my goats now. Probably Ahmed, that

I'm in Al-Qaeda

dick....
He won't treat them right.
I had the best goats anywhere along the Gomal River.
Beautiful Angoras.

WOMAN
People standing next to goats on my TV always look so poor. So desolate.

MAN
Goat herds need a pound of grain per goat per day—
or a good mixture of grasses.
Clean grasses and slightly warm water.
Goats are hearty but . . . persnickety.
The important thing is to try and keep them dry; a wet goat is a sick goat. And they need a worming every four weeks. That was my secret. My goats never had worms. No worms plus dry equals healthy goat. My goats show my love for Allah. Ahmed, that dick, has probably barbecued half of them and let the others fill with worms.

WOMAN
Your English is really good . . .

MAN
Oh, I have a Masters of Divinity from Harvard. God called me to be a goat herder.

WOMAN
That's rational.
How can you afford first class on a goat herder's salary?

MAN
Free upgrades. I spent 168 hours traveling last week,

and the week before, and the week before. And going back I don't know how long. Sometimes I land and there's snow. Sometimes not. I was sure it was summer, then I landed in a sleet storm. Then I realized that I had just flown American from Ft. Lauderdale to Anchorage. I don't know if it's summer or winter. It's always trying to be 72 degrees in airports. That same night, I eventually blacked out, probably from the tricresyl phosphate, while taking off from George Bush International Airport. I don't even know what city that's in.

WOMAN
Dallas.

MAN
Huh. I just assumed New England, since the family is from there.

WOMAN
That's just Prescott Bush.
But?

MAN
Oh, yesterday. United, from Atlanta to Vegas next to Rush Limbaugh's fact checker, Steve, then Sun Country, Vegas to Minneapolis next to some visiting scholar at the Humphrey Institute.
(beat)
I treated my goats well. I don't deserve this.

WOMAN
You must have more than a few goats. Be honest.

I'm in Al-Qaeda

MAN
(he's said this a million times)
I had nine goats. A shepherd's crook. A piece of flint. A small pocket knife. Six meters of rope and off-brand jeans, flip-flops, and a Buffalo Bills Super Bowl Champions 1992 T-shirt. I hate the Buffalo Airport so much.
(beat)
I'm very hungry.

WOMAN
It's first class. They'll feed us. And probably something good too.

MAN
No.

WOMAN
Yes. Everyone says they feed people in first class.

MAN
It won't be good.

WOMAN
?

MAN
It's a cross country flight on Delta, on a Wednesday. It's a barbecue pork sandwich.

WOMAN
Tasty.

MAN glares at her.

WOMAN *(Cont'd)*

What?

MAN

I just want to go home.

WOMAN

That's all?

MAN

I'd settle for blowing myself up in a café in Haifa.

Dark. End of play.

Whatsleeves

Justin Maxwell

Characters

SINGER: a strong performer with a weak grasp of irony.

Notes

The song is a William Burroughs style cut-up of "What Child Is This?" and "Greensleeves," a solemnly ridiculous conflation of religious and sexual love.

First produced as part of The Elm Theatre's The Naughty List in New Orleans, 2013.

Whatsleeves

*A **SINGER** bursts into a serious song.*

SINGER
What child is this, you do me wrong,
On Mary's lap discourteously.
For I have loved whom angels greet,
Delighting in your shepherds.

Greensleeves was all my joy
Whom shepherds guard and Angels sing.
Greensleeves was my heart of gold,
The Babe, the Son of Mary.

Such mean estate broken like my heart,
Where ox and ass so enrapture me?
Good Christians here in a world apart
The silent remains in captivity.

This, this is Christ the King,
Greensleeves was my delight.
Haste, haste, to bring Him laud,
And who but my lady greensleeves.

Nails, spear shall pierce your hand,
The cross for whatever you would crave,
I have both wagered the word made flesh,
Mary and good-will for to have.

This, this was all my joy
Greensleeves and Angels sing
Haste, haste was my heart of gold
And who but my lady Mary.
If you intend incense, gold and myrrh,
come peasant to enrapture me,
And even so salvation brings

loving hearts in captivity.

Greensleeves was Christ the King,
Whom shepherds guard for my delight
Greensleeves was to bring Him laud
The Babe, the my lady greensleeves.

Ah, Greensleeves, now farewell oh high
To God I pray her lullaby,
Joy, joy thy lover true,
Come once again Mary.

End of play.

$\sim 6x^3 = \text{SAFETY}$

a comedic list poem

Justin Maxwell

Character

WOMAN: one body, multiple manifestations.

Notes

While one performer plays all the roles, she becomes five different characters, each independent of the other.

First produced as part of Tiny Theater! Festival by The Brick and the Ontological Hysteric Theaters in New York City, 2008.

~6x³=SAFETY

*At rise, a **WOMAN** in a 6x6x6 cube frame, made of piping, and containing an assortment of building materials inside. The **WOMAN** will construct a 5x5x5 PVC cube suspended from the larger one, while she speaks. This is a cube made of detail.*

WOMAN

You've really got to watch out for the fucking plovers. I mean it. The semipalmated plover will turn your stove on when you're not home. The snowy plover likes to distract you while you're driving. The Eurasian Dotterel has been known to steal your important handbooks. And the killdeer . . . well, the killdeer will kill your deer. Just that simple. Of course the plovers are saints compared to the mimids: The gray catbird enjoys violating the UN Declaration of Human Rights. The brown thrasher will damage your plumbing, and it is in your house right now. And for the love of Christ, don't get me started on the flycatchers. My shrink suggested that I'm agoraphobic.

(beat)

But it's important to be detail oriented. It is. It's important for one's safety. Sense of safety, my shrink would say, but fuck him. Last week he had an egg-shaped bruise on his left forearm. Said he walked into a doorknob. But I think we all know . . . . Lacks. Detail. Attention. No safety there. So I came home from Dr. Doorknob's and painted all my windows blaze orange. Think about it. A razor tipped hunting arrow could just come smashing through at any moment and poke me in the spleen, or a miscellaneous gland of some type, because my living room accent wall is green, and a hunter with bad depth perception could think there's more woods in here. I'm not over-reacting. There's a big hedge below the picture window. So this is possible. Shrubbery occurs naturally in nature you know—it's an undeniable fact. Go ahead. Try and deny it. I'll wait. See? Undeniable. And a stray arrow to the spleen is exactly how my cousin Jeany died. Plus, now the birds can't watch me with their beady, watchy-eyes always looking out for stray hair to weave into their nests. I fucking hate those greedy songbirds. Fucking nuthatch. Fucking house wren. Fucking tufted titmouse. Fucking phoebe. The way they all stare at me with their eyes. They sit on their branches and stare at me right through my windows. I always hoped a stray arrow would take care of them. But, no such luck. They could do anything with all the staring. See you naked. Learn your best recipes and upstage you at the church bake sale.

> *The **WOMAN** has an epiphany.*
>
> *The **WOMAN** becomes a completely different character. She notices the building materials and as she talks to us she begins to construct a 4x4x4 cube inside the cube she's currently in; it is made of leadership.*

WOMAN
(manifesto-like)
I became a kindergarten teacher because I wanted to make the world a better place: A safe place.
I became a kindergarten teacher because children are our most precious resource.
I became a kindergarten teacher because our most precious resource would never hold any kind of meaningful inquisition into your life.

$\sim 6x^3 = SAFETY$

because . . .
   because . . .
      because . . .
Because seventh graders are all bastards, asking questions about boob jobs and everything.
Because a kindergartener will never write the phrase "donkey dick" in the margin of a multiple choice test.
Because if a kindergartener goes through your purse, they have no idea what they're looking at and they won't fuck with your stuff.
Because kindergarteners haven't learned that their culture hates women.
Because you can go fuck yourself!
Because kindergarteners are two dimensional narcissists, but they're cute two dimensional narcissists.
I became a kindergarten teacher because . . .
   because of the wonderful things he does.

> *The **WOMAN** shifts to a new persona and begins to build a smaller cube, 3x3x3. It is made of self-righteousness.*

WOMAN

One can know nothing about John Milton, born 1608, died 1674.

If one uses conditional statements one can safely deduce life-altering facts.

If you put a hat on Milton's skull, before the museum guards get to you, you'll find he wears a seven and seven-eighths fedora—see the photo in appendix B.

If you read stanza four of Milton's "On the Morning of Christ's Nativity," you'll see that Milton was secretly obsessed with stink.

If you pick the Schlage lock on the back of the Milton

Justin Maxwell

Museum in London, you can sneak in and touch Milton's . . . books.

If you touch Milton's books just right, you'll understand "On the Morning of Christ's Nativity."

If you touch Milton's books, then you've touched Josephus's *Antiquities of the Jews* and his *Tractatus Effluvium*, and Eusebius of Caesarea's *History of the Church*, and Xenophon's *The Persian Baths*, and Saint Abra Cadabara's *Whichever Way the Wind Blows: The Olfactory Implications of Roman Public Execution.*

It you read the books concurrently, by flashlight, you'll understand the first two lines of "Christ's Nativity": "See how far upon the eastern road / the star-led wizards haste with odours sweet,"

If you get the aforementioned lines, then you haven't been watching too much television.

If you haven't been watching too much television, then you're probably not overweight and understand why Milton is important.

If you're not overweight then you must understand the next two lines: "O run, prevent them with thy humble ode, / And lay it lowly at his blessed feet;"

And if you know anything about whatever, then you know that "ode" is a 17th Century colloquialism for odor. If you know about ancient colloquialisms, then you understand Bethlehem. And you know that Bethlehem must have stunk from the crucified locals and the results of a porcine disease Josephus refers to only as "pig pox."

If you know about "pig pox," then you're really on to something there.

If you're really onto something there, then you'll be able to engage the deeper meaning of the last lines: "Have thou the honour first thy Lord to greet, / And join thy

voice unto the angel choir, / From out his secret altar touched with hallowed fire."
If you see the deeper meaning of these lines then you know this is an allusion to Isaiah, chapter six, verses six and seven.
If you know Isaiah,
then you can give me a ride home after the conference.

> *The **WOMAN** shifts personas again and begins work on a 2x2x2 cube; it is made of hermeticism.*
>
> *The following monologue is delivered flatly, yet she seems to nail the interview.*

WOMAN

I'd like to start off by expressing my sincere excitement over the opportunity to interview for this position. For someone like myself this is a rare opportunity to escape academia and really apply my work in quantum geometry, and with the funding available at Lockheed Martin I really hope to bring some amazing breakthroughs to the company.
 (she listens to a question)
I have to disagree. The University system isn't safe at all. Safety comes from successful research, and successful research is well-supported research, and well-supported research takes the pockets of private industry or military contracts. Or both.
 (she laughs, a flat and forced sound—ridiculous)
Yes. *Quod Erat Demonstrandum.*
 (listens)
Well, because of my work's inherently cutting-edge nature, it's hard to talk about specific applications. I think it's better to understand it paradigmatically. Manifes-

tations of the geometries I explore have implications to everything your company develops.
(listens)
It's an experience I'm looking forward to. It'll be nice to work in a spirit of collaboration rather than competition.
(listens)
A formula in the title usually lets readers know if the math is plausible before they even start to read the research.
(listens)
No, whenever I asked, I was told that Doctor Benway was on sabbatical.
(listens)
A heliocentric solar system was science fiction once too. At its heart I'm exploring how matter and energy can still have simple, Newtonian relationships but without direct, causal contact with each other.
(listens)
Oh, the occasional drink after work with the girls . . . .
(listens)
Really, I'd be the only . . . okay: the occasional drink after work with the boys.
(listens)
That's not a problem for the salary you're offering, Jack. I mean, Dr. Off.
(listens)
I already speak Mandarin. Well, I'm not fluent, but I've got the basics.
(listens)
I just assumed that would be a prerequisite, so . . . yes.
(listens)
No. I'm not familiar with anything called Project Mugwump.

(listens)

No. I've never had any symptoms of altitude sickness.
(listens)

That depends. Do you mean military volunteers like test pilots, who are well-paid for their work?
(listens)

Yes. I think that's perfectly ethical.
(listens)

I'm not sure I follow you . . . .
(listens)

Yes. Oh, now I understand. Yes, this is weapons-grade geometry.

(She smiles at her sudden revelation, but not the next one.)

*The **WOMAN** transforms yet again and begins a new cube, now 1x1x1. By the end of the last monologue the **WOMAN**'s head is inside the last cube as though she were on TV. It is a cube made of empty pleasure.*

WOMAN

No one ever suspects the geese.

A bird in the hand is worth somewhere between 4.87 and 5.02, unless it's a ring neck pheasant.

The safety demonstration must be repeated until we are all safe.

Blood is thicker than water, when it's four degrees Celsius or warmer.

Cat got your untoward sense of masculinity?

Now with trans fats. Or without trans fats. Something, something trans fats.

Don't look a gift horse in the genitals, until its previous owner is completely out of the barn.

Justin Maxwell

Boys will be boys; what choice do they have?
And if I die before I wake, I pray the Lord my soul to take.
My education can never be taken away from me—unless I get a head wound, or just forget stuff.
In case of fire, use stairs.
This year's cabbage festival was equally as memorable as the previous year's.
Our local bird watcher hasn't seen a goddamn thing all goddamn day.
Our dinner theater production of *Titus Andronicus* failed to increase dessert orders.
We installed a "tornado warning siren" during the Cold War.
Our prophet of disaster was right for once.
The plow is unforgivable.
Objects in mirror are closer than they appear.
This chrestomathy is superior to the last chrestomathy.
The safety demonstration must be repeated until we are all safe.
Aphorisms are as effective as similes.
Our 24-hour news cycle continues unabated.
Scientists are researching a cure.
Your video is buffering.
I am innocent of everything you've proven I've done.
Keep in mind, emergency exits may be located behind you.
This is all you get. No seconds.
The maximum capacity of this elevator is 1,100 pounds.
Why do my scented candles always reek of failure?
Crumple zones.
No lifeguard on duty.
Choking hazard.
May contain nuts.

$\sim 6x^3 = SAFETY$

Does this box make my head look fat?
The safety demonstration must be repeated.
The safety demonstration must be.
The safety demonstration must

She snaps her fingers. Sudden dark. End of play.

Justin Maxwell

My Rich Temple

Justin Maxwell

Characters

PYTHIA: an oracle burdened by the problems of heaven and earth.

LYCURGUS: a king with a problem.

HERA: a god that makes problems.

APHRODITE: a god, no more problematic than any other.

APOLLO: a god, no more problematic than any other.

ZEUS: a problematic god.

Setting

Delphi, about 555 BCE.

First produced as part of the Master Works Series by Commedia Beauregard in Minneapolis, 2010.

My Rich Temple

*At rise, a woman of mighty countenance, the **PYTHIA**, stands down stage in a spotlight, holding a jar of ether. She appears to be in a trance-like state and speaks in a great voice—its power is awesome, divine. **LYCURGUS** speaks from off stage.*

*The gods speak through the **PYTHIA** and have intense, if not exact, control over her body; she is a puppet for several drunken puppeteers.*

PYTHIA
Is it you, Lycurgus, that comes to my rich temple?

LYCURGUS
(Shocked that she knows his name.)
Yes. I come from Sparta. My name is . . . well . . . yes . . . . We ask for laws, for a code of conduct to govern our state. We have nothing but fear and suffering. Please help us.

PYTHIA
(Having completely ignored him.)
Lycurgus, dear to Zeus and to all that hold the halls of Olympus?

LYCURGUS
Yes, well, yes, I think so.

PYTHIA
I ask myself whether, in prophecy, as a god or a man I shall hail you.

LYCURGUS
Man?

Justin Maxwell

> *Lights up to reveal Olympus, a place that looks much like an upscale Manhattan apartment, but cloudy. It is early morning; **HERA**, **ZEUS**, **APOLLO**, and **APHRODITE** are profoundly drunk. **HERA** is whispering the words the **PYTHIA** is speaking. The others are trying to control their snickering, which **LYCURGUS** can not hear.*

PYTHIA and HERA
(whispering simultaneously)
Nay but 'tis rather a god that I see in you, Lycurgus.

APHRODITE
'Tis rather a god? Shit. Who says that?

LYCURGUS
Well, I don't know . . . .

APOLLO
The things you put my priest through.

ZEUS
*(While speaking, makes an obscene gesture which the **PYTHIA** mimics.)*
You get the initiation ceremonies.

HERA
She's a virgin. Get over it.

> ***HERA** turns her attention back to the prophet; **HERA** whispers, and the prophet speaks with slightly glazed-over eyes. **HERA**'s drunken attempts at using her hands for emphasis become gesticulations of madness and hilarity when copied by the **PYTHIA**.*

HERA
I will now dictate unto you

PYTHIA
I will now dictate unto you

HERA
the laws of a great state

PYTHIA
the laws of a great state

HERA
which you shall build,

PYTHIA
which you shall build,

HERA
cutie.

PYTHIA
Prophet!

LYCURGUS
I, I'll do what I can but

ZEUS
(Drunker than the rest.)
I said SILENCE!

PYTHIA
(Mimics his motions.)
Silence!

ZEUS
Lycurgus, father of Sparta

PYTHIA
Lycurgus, father of Sparta

ZEUS
Since you're here, where is your good looking wife?

APHRODITE
Jerk.

HERA
Enough! These are the laws that shall govern the Lacedaemonians.

PYTHIA
These are the laws that shall govern the Lacedaemonians.

ZEUS
Who?

APOLLO
The Spartans.

ZEUS
Who? Why the crap do they have two names?

APHRODITE
(flippant)
Why not? Every time some unwashed mother fucker builds us a temple they slap a little something local

onto us, like we're going to get all worked up over how they made us a special necklace of bronzed cow shit or whatever.

APOLLO
What?

HERA
The First Law of Sparta, to be delivered by Lycurgus shall be. . .
that. . .
um, shall be that Spartans are to. . .

APHRODITE
Exercise. It's the best thing you can do for yourself.

ZEUS
They should be strong people.

APOLLO
Orderly.

PYTHIA
Spartans are to be a strong and orderly people.

APHRODITE
And well groomed.

ZEUS
I like sexy hair.

PYTHIA
Well groomed, especially the hair.

HERA
The Second Law of Sparta shall be that they must always be . . .

PYTHIA
The Second Law of Sparta shall be that they must always be very highly organized.

APHRODITE
The women must be as great as the men.

ZEUS
Who will give up on the women all together.

APOLLO
Have them all live in separate huts.

HERA
Tell him the law Pythia.

*The **PYTHIA** takes a hit of ether then speaks.*

PYTHIA
(Guessing.)
There shall be two kings to rule Sparta. They will each get a double ration of food and special seats at the annual games. If they are wealthy they may stay wealthy. Otherwise . . . nothing special.

APHRODITE
I love my husband.

APOLLO
We all watched you fuck Aries.

My Rich Temple

APHRODITE
By love, I meant: I'm married to him.

HERA
The Sixth Law of Sparta shall be

ZEUS
You've only given them two.

APOLLO
I thought it was three.

HERA
This is six!

APHRODITE
We should create a variety of fashion statutes. And rules around total celibacy for the ugly ones. We don't need any superfluous breeding.

ZEUS
And they should do it all together, on their rooftops.

HERA
*(Pointing at the **PYTHIA** drunkenly.)*
OK, Pythia, go for it.

PYTHIA
(Points wildly.)
All the Spartans shall come together, take their meals together, prepare for war, and make themselves beautiful.

HERA
Oh, that's very good.

APOLLO
She didn't get that right at all.

ZEUS
She did fine, little cutie.

APHRODITE
I don't know about that. Look at that get-up. Who came up with that costume anyway?

APOLLO
I did.

ZEUS explodes into laughter.

HERA
I think it's role-appropriate, and I'm especially glad you didn't make her wear lots of gold, or carry a stylized lyre.

APOLLO
She's not carrying the stylized lyre?

HERA
We have laws to dictate.

PYTHIA takes a big hit of ether.

APHRODITE
Quit sniveling, you three are as bad as that Persephone bitch. Did we really need winter? No. It's completely stupid. Winter requires one to divide their time and attention between multiple wardrobes. But does she care? No. Little-Miss-Fashion-Doesn't-Change-In-The-Un-

My Rich Temple

derworld should just stay down there. Have a few more pomegranate seeds honey.

ZEUS

Mortals don't have the scope for real problems. Remember I had to eat the entire universe once.
(singing)
Nobody knows the trouble I've seen . . .

HERA

They could build one of us a nice statue.

APHRODITE

(Gestures to breasts and nose.)
Please, they never get my breasts right. And that nose, really.

PYTHIA

*(Copying **APHRODITIE**'s gestures)*
The oracle of Delphi favors you Lycurgus, remember to heap honors upon its gods and you will be rewarded with good augury. The gods give you good laws; do not forget their alms.

HERA

She is good at this. Shame she'll die in another twenty years or so.

ZEUS

Or lose her virginity.

APHRODITE

Is that really such a big deal?

APOLLO
Has to be a virgin. Otherwise they get too distracted with their own lives and

> ***APOLLO** makes a sexually suggestive gesture with his pelvis—**PYTHIA** mimics it.*

APOLLO *(Cont'd)*
don't bother with me enough.

HERA
Pythia, just tell the Spartans the rest of the laws for me. If you do a good job I'll have Apollo let you spend the rest of the day huffing ether.

> ***PYTHIA** takes a huge hit of ether.*

APHRODITE
You don't stop being a pig do you?

HERA
He really doesn't. I torment every mortal that he gets an interest in, and it does next to nothing.

ZEUS
I've got some ideas.

HERA
Not a chance. OK. Pythia. Here we go.

> ***PYTHIA** huffs into a "trance," mimicking as **HERA** dictates dramatically.*

HERA
Lycurgus, or whatever, birth-father of a great law-abiding gaggle

PYTHIA
Lycurgus, birth-father of a great law-abiding people

HERA
follow these things and your gaggle shall grow irrevocably, except for those who die, and other such personages

PYTHIA
obey the laws given to you by the gods and Sparta shall prosper

HERA
unless they fuck-up, or there's a plague or something

PYTHIA
greater than its lawless neighbors.

HERA
She's so good at this. They shall forever strive to be a people of strong, brave, more equitable brutality.

PYTHIA
They shall be a society of equals, brave, strong, able to withstand brutality.

APHRODITE
In nice uniforms, but lets avoid ostentation.

HERA
Those two kings we'll have 'em be generals really with,

you know, subsets, smaller and smaller units. But still equal or whatever.

PYHTIA

The forth law of Sparta shall be that the kings rule equally. One shall go off to fight, bringing those soldiers that he needs. The people will be divided up militarily, with a clear, orderly chain of command. In Sparta both kings are in charge and must always consider the opinions of the ruling families, i.e. elders, i.e. generals. When one king is waging war,

ZEUS

The details are their problem.

PYTHIA

winning land, slaves, and honor for Sparta. The other king will stay at home.

ZEUS

Stay at home like a woman!

PYTHIA

Run the state . . . efficiently.

HERA

She's so good at this.
(beat)
Murderers, weaklings out! Dues to pay for army shit, but no taxes. Think long-term.

APHRODITE

All work and no play?

HERA

And remember to have a little fun once in a while, let your hair down, or whatever. And don't let too many people join up. You'll get a bunch of slackers mooching off your hard work.

PYTHIA
(Overwhelmed, huffs.)
Finally. Keep allies close but only the strongest and those who pay their dues on time can be members. Anyone who misses a payment . . . out. So you might not want to get too expensive there but you get the idea. And remember that games and holidays are sacred to the gods who favor you, honor and respect these traditions as you have been honored and respected today.

*Lights fade out, first Olympus and then the **PYTHIA**. Just as darkness descends:*

HERA

Oh, that's good stuff.

End of play.

Justin Maxwell

Old MacDonald Dirge

Justin Maxwell

The limits of my language mean the limits of my world.
>   —Ludwig Wittgenstein, *Tractatus Logico-Philosophicus*

Justin Maxwell

Characters

SINGER: a child.

Notes

The child sings a variation of "Old MacDonald Had a Farm." It is performed to the usual tune but done at about a fourth or so of the usual speed so that each verse takes about thirty seconds. In other words, dirge tempo. The more dirge-like the better. However, there is enough material here for an actor to modify the performance to fit their personal style.

First produced at the Freshwater Theatre Festival of Awkward Moments in Minneapolis, 2011.

Old MacDonald Dirge

*A spotlight reveals a small, serious child, the **SINGER**, a soloist in some kind of grade school program complete with cheesy plywood animals and farm stuff.*

*The **SINGER** becomes progressively sadder as the song progresses and is openly crying by the end. The work becomes funnier the slower and sadder it is performed—this is fun with schadenfreude.*

SINGER

Old MacDonald had a farm
E-I-E-I-O
And on this farm he had a horse
E-I-E-I-O
And this horse its name was puppy
E-I-E-I-O

Old MacDonald had a farm
E-I-E-I-O
And on this farm he had a cow
E-I-E-I-O
And this cow its name was puppy
E-I-E-I-O

Old MacDonald had a farm
E-I-E-I-O
And on this farm he had a lamb
E-I-E-I-O
And this lamb its name was puppy
E-I-E-I-O

Old MacDonald had a farm
E-I-E-I-O

Justin Maxwell

And on this farm he had a pig
E-I-E-I-O
And this pig its name was puppy
E-I-E-I-O

Old MacDonald had a farm
E-I-E-I-O
And on this farm he had a duck
E-I-E-I-O
And this duck its name was puppy
E-I-E-I-O

Old MacDonald had a farm
E-I-E-I-O
And on this farm he had a veal calf
E-I-E-I-O
And this veal calf its name was puppy
E-I-E-I-O

Lights down to dark. End of play.

Patience on the Way to Daylight

an *Ars Poetica* farce

Justin Maxwell

Cast

Three (any age, any gender).

Running time

Nine minutes.

Location

A strange place.

Notes

The characters, generally, talk *fast*; the slower this goes overall, the worse it will sound—pacing and timing are everything for this to work. As part of the timing that drives this play, the dialog is currently unassigned, and the director and actors should be free to discover who says what as the work goes into rehearsal to give them the necessary ownership of the material.

The show was originally written for the Minneapolis-based company Commedia Beauregard, in 2010, as part of their Masterworks Series, which has a playwright "translate" a work of visual art into a performance. The painting that I translated was Orlando Leibovitz's untitled painting often referred to as "Modern Times Painting 1." It can be viewed most easily on his web page: http://www.orlandoleibovitz.com/ModernTimes1.html. The image should be projected for the audience at/before the beginning of the show.

First produced as part of the Master Works Series by Commedia Beauregard in Minneapolis, 2010.

Patience on the Way to Daylight

The image of Orlando Leibovitz's "Modern Times Painting 1" comes up, holds, then fades.

Lights rise to reveal: Three people wrapped in black, mummy-like wrappings, berets, goggles, and wearing harnesses of the appropriate color. Each stands on a box of different heights. Ideally, lights will shine up at them, as well as down from the grid.

I'm a philosopher.
You can tell by the parachute.
I'm a gorgon.
You can tell by the snakes.
I'm terrified. You can tell by the terror.
What are we doing here?
Why aren't we falling?
How do you know we're not falling?
I'm pretty sure I'm falling.
No, you'd have hit me by now.
I'm pretty sure I'm falling.
Maybe we're all falling at the exact same speed.
We don't have any objects for perspective.
We have evenly spaced horizontal lines.
Oh. Yes.
Maybe this is some kind of stasis?
What, like a force field?
No. Like an unchanging situation.
Do you think we're stuck like this?
Maybe.
It's . . . safe here. It feels kinda safe like this.
Safe? This looks like a nightmare.
What can you see from over there?
It seems to be lighter below.

Justin Maxwell

That's odd. The sun should be above us.
I'm clearly underlit. You?
Yes. Me too.
We're lit from two directions at once.
That's bad.
Probably causes cancer.
Shut up. Light does not cause cancer.
Skin cancer.
Shut up.
Maybe that's why we can't tell if we're falling.
Are you sure the sky is lit from below?
No. It's surprisingly complicated to tell what I'm looking at.
I can see my house from here!
Really?
No. But how often do you get to say it?
I miss my house.
Maybe I could see mine. It shows up at the most unexpected times.
It's hard to tell with these blinders on.
And the sensory deprivation suits . . . .
Deprivation suits? Shit. I was hoping we were fashionistas.
No, we're philosophers.
(a bit sad) Pretty sure I'm a gorgon.
Maybe you're the only philosopher here.
Are you sure we're not falling?
Wait. I'm still uncertain if we can see or not.
I think I'm probably Sthenno—one of the immortal gorgons.
How did we get into these contraptions anyway?
It seems as though I'd remember putting on a big green harness.
I agree. Well . . . purple harness. But still.

Patience on the Way to Daylight

Still.
It *seems* like we *should* be falling. What, with the parachutes and everything.
The grid still isn't moving.
Maybe the grid is the wrong thing to worry about.
We should be falling *towards* the earth.
Which isn't really a light source.
Exactly.
Maybe that explains the wrapping.
Is this stuff asbestos?
God damn it!
I don't know.
Does it feel itchy? I think asbestos would be itchy.
It feels itchy now.
This black lip gloss doesn't seem particularly organic either.
    (licks lips)
God. Don't lick it.
Okay. Look. Let's not think about the outfits.
The light is pretty uniform.
Good.
Good?
Yeah. If it were light from a burning city or a lava flow or some shit it wouldn't be so even.
The light has stasis too.
Weird.
So what is it?
The fact that we can see it through these blinders is pretty alarming.
You know, *(touches goggles)* I think these might be welder's goggles.
That's not good.
No.
What *is* that?

Justin Maxwell

Maybe it doesn't matter what it is?
We don't seem to be getting any closer or any further away.
And we don't seem to be falling.
What is that down there?
It's alarming.
I don't mean: "What is that?" in the abstract.
Maybe we should be more concerned with the stasis than the light source?
    (an unspoken revelation)
What if . . . instead of falling into that light, what if, nothing happens?
We just stay like this?
Yes.
Oh.
That's worse.
    (a long beat)
What if we unwrap the asbestos bandages?
What about the parachutes?
Best to leave them on for now.
    (one of them unwraps a finger)
Okay. That's not too bad.
You sure?
No.
Falling?
(waves naked finger) Doesn't feel like it. *(unwraps a little more)*
Hmmm?
(unwraps the bandages further) Oh. *(itches the exposed part)* Oh. That's so much better. You two should try this.
    (one does, one doesn't)
I think I'll wait and see how it works out for you both.

    One takes all the wrappings and the goggles off, ideally naked, if the actor doesn't wimp out about it. The other partially unwraps. The third doesn't move. Just watches.

How do you feel?
Good.
A little, well, exposed. But good.
I'm taking off this harness too. *(removes harness)*
I'm going to keep mine.
You know what. I am a gorgon. *(the naked one exits)*
That seems a bit much. But *(sits comfortably)* I'm going to keep my eye on whatever the hell that light is.
Indeed.
Hey, is that my house?

Dark. End of play.

Justin Maxwell

Exhausted Paint

the Death of Van Gogh

Justin Maxwell

Characters

VINCENT VAN GOGH: a great painter.

Notes

The show is built around ideas of disorientation and struggle. These are exemplified by a single set piece. The piece is a horizontal wheel on a post, parallel to the stage, and mounted on an axle so that it can be spun by the actor. From the rim of the wheel hangs a series of objects (mobile-like), each of which denotes a scene of the play. After the initial scene, the actor will spin the wheel and perform the scene appropriate to that object. Consequently, the play doesn't have a set internal structure, only the introduction and finale are set. The other scenes can happen in any order.

Also, there should be some wine available for the performer. He'll need a glass of it for "Scene: Rag" and with all the talking the poor actor has to do, something to drink is a good idea. Water works too, as does bringing enough wine for the whole audience. As a side note, grape juice tends to make a terrible substitute.

The date listed in the first line of "Scene: Introduction" is a place holder and should be replaced by the date of the current production. Similarly, the name "Shawn," in "Scene: Light," is a placeholder for Shawn Boyd, the actor who first performed the role. His name should be replaced by the name of whoever is performing the show.

The play happens in a single spotlight, which has the axle of the wheel at its center point. The show works best in a cabaret setting where the actor can get very close to audience members.

First produced as part of the Chicago Fringe Festival, 2010.

Scene: Introduction

Spotlight up to reveal the wheel. ***VAN GOGH*** *enters, slight bump in houselights so the actor can see the audience a bit.*

VAN GOGH

It's September 1, 2010, and I'm more popular than ever.
Because I am dead you can do whatever you want with me, and I can't object.
You might as well,
you did the same thing when I was alive.
Thousands of people visit my home every year.
Millions buy reproductions of my work and yearn after the originals.
Billions of people recognize my canvases.
And I need to say to you all:
> Fuck off.

Where were you when I was making three paintings a day?
Where were you when I went crazy?
Where were you when I was sick?
Had you come through for me when I needed you, I would have made the world a richer place.
You never had a chance to know Vincent Van Gogh, and you don't have one now.
Van Gogh the painter is just a contrivance for a different artist to make a piece of art—repurposing me is a long tradition that includes Antonin Artaud and Martin Heidegger.
Now I'm just a character in a play.
Again.
At least this actor looks like me. Kinda.

Justin Maxwell

But his French is fucking terrible. And his Dutch is worse.

> ***VAN GOGH*** *goes to the wheel. On it, front and center to the audience, is a black square, probably the back of a painting.* ***VAN GOGH*** *removes the square. The expectation is that he'll reveal what's on the other side.*

I could say, let me paint you a picture. But I won't. I live before irony, and you live after it. So, clearly, I'm having some identity issues. Some people look at my work and think I'm crazy. Or that I'm an artistic genius and that we're all like this. Others read my letters and think I'm depressed, or manic, or alcoholic, or that I've got O.C.D. Others hypothesize that I've got an inner ear disorder. No shit. Inner ear. They think I'm just a guy who wanted to paint and that had a screwed up cochlea. Their theory is my favorite. When I was at the asylum at Saint Remy, they didn't look at my ears once.
So, here's the question:
What happens when you reach for the brass ring and miss?
   (This is building to a reveal . . .)
At the end of my life, there are about ten people who are impressed by my art. In hindsight, they really came through for me. In the moment, not so much. There's an anecdote that says I only sold one painting in my whole life. It's good for an anecdote. But.
They never seemed to understand my works are *very* ordered, very consciously created.
I could explain every brushstroke
on every canvas,
every lively daub of paint had intention.

Exhausted Paint

Art I could control,
success I could not.
So,
I need to tell you the story of my failure.
All the times I reached and missed,
reached and missed.
I need to show you something about disorder.

>   ***VAN GOGH*** *turns over the black square to reveal: nothing. It is black on the other side too! He places it on the ground. He spins the wheel. Whichever scene-object stops towards the audience is the scene that's performed next.*

Justin Maxwell

Scene: Gun

The gun has come up on the wheel. **VAN GOGH** *removes it, careful not to hold it as a weapon.*

VAN GOGH

Since you have the wherewithal to be in a theater today—good choice by the way—you probably know the rule: If there's a gun on stage in act one it better go off by act three. I think this comes from Chekhov, but I don't really keep up on such things. Or guns in general, really. In nearly a thousand letters I never mention guns. Not once. And I do some high-risk stuff in my private life . . . . I drink, a lot. Absinthe. I drink turpentine on one occasion. I smoke. Not American-trying-to-quite, smoke. I mean 19th Century, European, artist smoke. I have unprotected sex with prostitutes. Often. I spend a lot of time outside in burning sun and freezing rain. I spend time inside in poorly heated apartments. I'm poor. All the high-risk stuff. Oh, and those apartments are poorly ventilated and filled with the fumes of dozens of square yards of curing oil paint—of all the theories for my "condition," nobody has mentioned huffing, yet.

(to an audience member.)

You, you know what I mean.

I mention these things in my letters. Hell, I advocate these things in my letters. Well, not the turpentine. That was a terrible decision. But every other self-destructive thing. All that, and I never mention guns. Or suicide. Fortunately, this is a one-act; it's short. No third act. No inevitable gun play.

(to the same audience member.)

Relieved? Good.

Just to be safe, I want you to hold this for me.

VAN GOGH gives the gun to the same audience member. He spins the wheel.

Scene: Potato

The potato has come up on the wheel. **VAN GOGH** *removes it and takes a little nibble of the raw potato. Yes, it's fine to eat them like that. As this scene goes on,* **VAN GOGH** *takes progressively more dramatic bites from the potato, wolfing it down by the end.*

VAN GOGH
So, as an adolescent, I started fooling with painting for all the bullshit, romantic reasons that a boy goes in for art: vanity, laziness, selfishness, the hope that chicks will dig it. They don't by the way. But some really go for vanity and laziness and selfishness. So, when painting started to get . . . hard, when I hit that point where I was going to have to give some serious suffering to it, I became a priest instead. Kinda. It's a moment some of you musicians have experienced, when, seemingly at random or just when you were sure you were going to make it your bassist, or drummer, or whoever quits the band to go back to community college. You've been there. Me, I read the Bible. I mean, read it a lot.
    (Suddenly tent revival preacher, just while eating a potato.)
Brothers and sisters—
Can I get an Amen?
    (If no one does.)
I said: Can I get an amen, motherfuckers?
    (If/when they do.)
I read from the Bible.
I read Corinthians.
I read Matthew.
I read Revelations.

Justin Maxwell

I read the whole black-bound thing.
And I was filled with the good news.
Filled with the light and
filled with the life of
Jesus H. Christ Almighty himself.
And I heard my calling. I would take the good word to the people.
I read them the sermon on the mount;
I knew the meek had a big inheritance coming.
Had I been an American, I'd have toured the Middle West in a tent and made some serious money.
(Down. Out of preacher character.)
But, I'm Dutch.
We don't tour.
No chance to fingerbang buxom, corn-fed girls behind the tents at the county fair.
My people were peasants. Old school, Euro-peasants. Folks who harvested barley with hand scythes, and who had been doing so for a thousand years. American farmers work on the very top of the earth. Peasants *are* the earth, buried deep in the soil. Generations scythed away as oak tress grew up, withered, died, and grew again. Those peasants were buried in the dirt of their farms for so long they are its dirt, and its produce, and its workers, and its dirt, ad infinitum. And I love them. So I needed to tell them about the Bible. I mean they already knew everything they needed to know, and everything they wanted to know. But I . . .
(beat)
I needed to *tell* them.
I got a few gigs as an assistant pastor.
I gave a few sermons.
And I was doing important work.
Work that could have kept me close to the peasants I

claim to cherish so.
But it didn't sustain me.
So a sketch here and there, a family, an idea for a painting, another sketch,
a nude or two,
and suddenly the peasants didn't want me around. And the Catholic priests told people to avoid me.
(Offers bite of potato to audience member.)
So I went off to learn painting at the foot of a Dutch master.
I tucked my evangelical tail between my legs and . . . hell.
I cut that tail clean off.

    VAN GOGH *spins the wheel.*

Justin Maxwell

Exhausted Paint

Scene: Rag

The rag has come up on the wheel. ***VAN GOGH*** *looks at it—a quiet trauma.*

VAN GOGH
So I fail in Paris. A combination of poverty, cold, heat, and expensive hookers exhausts me. I get a great fatigue. Or maybe depression. Or syphilis. Or, maybe, artistic temperament of some kind. It will return. And return, and return.

> ***VAN GOGH*** *waggles his ear; then he takes the rag from the wheel and snaps it taunt.*

I move to Arles in Southern France, for the light. And the warmth. And I try to bring the other Impressionists with me. You'd call it an artist's colony nowadays. I just called it survival.
   (beat)
Fuck.
It's never been about survival. If I wanted an artist's colony I'd have been an organizer, but I'm not an organizer. Or at least not a good one. I'm a painter. My brother loves art like I do. But he *gets* survival. Although, ironically, he also gets what the doctors call neurosyphilis and dies a year after me. But, before his whole death thing, he was about survival. He did well enough as an art dealer to support a family, and even before that he did well enough to support me. I'd have painted and starved and vanished from the world in sixty days if it wasn't for him. By the time I'd get around to thinking about survival, I'd, hell . . .
my last thought probably would have been:

Justin Maxwell

How long have I been this hungry? Before collapsing on my easel.
> *(Wrings rag, stressed.)*

My brother sends me money every month.
I fantasize about that.
> I perseverate about it.
>> I worm and twitch from it.

Each franc is given with love and heavy with guilt.
Each tube of paint he sent, each brush, each letter—
he loved me in a way I can't understand. We were an odd little threesome. He loved me, I loved painting; we both loved art, which didn't care a whit.
And I . . . I can't make the world work.
Eventually, I get Gauguin to come and live with me, in my two bedroom "artist's colony." We have great talks about art.
I say things like: "The peculiar effects of perspective intrigue me more than human intrigues."
And he says "blah blah, blah blah, naked Tahitians."
I say: "Cobalt—is a divine colour and there is nothing as fine for putting atmosphere around things. Carmine is the red of wine and is warm and lively like wine. The same goes for emerald green too. It's false economy to dispense with them, with those colours. Cadmium as well."
Then I say: "For instead of trying to reproduce exactly what I see before me, I make more arbitrary use of colour to express myself more forcefully."
Then I get carried away. Soliloquy carried away:
> *(A parody of himself.)*

"I shall be an obstinate colourist. I shall exaggerate the fairness of the hair, arrive at tones of orange, chrome, pale yellow. Behind the head—instead of painting an ordinary wall of the shabby apartment, I shall paint infinity, I shall do a simple background of the richest, most intense blue that I can contrive, and by this simple combination, the shining fair head against this rich blue background, I shall obtain a mysterious effect, like a star in the deep blue sky."

Then Gauguin says: "I *should like* to do portraits which will appear as revelations to people in a hundred years' time."

Well, okay, I said that last one too. He really said "blah, blah, blah, blah, nearby brothel, good wine." After all, he was one of the great geniuses of his generation.

In general, that's an exact transcription of all our conversations. Except I made up Gauguin's part. And my parts are actually excerpts from my letters to my brother. And it was all done in Dutch. And translated by Arnold Pomerans. And misappropriated by Justin Maxwell. But other than that, flawlessly accurate.

This completes the colony. One Gauguin, one me.

Our discussions became fights, since I couldn't ever get his "point of view," even though I listened carefully to each blah he blah-blahhed. And he was one of my closest friends. And I did admire him so. And I

(Angry.)

I needed him to see my ideas about art were RIGHT. Just, *right*. His were good. His were genius even. Mine were right. Eventually, everything became ritual.

He drops the rag. Sits crossed legged. Picks up the rag. Drops it again. His actions are like a Zen tea ceremony.

I had a point to make.

He takes the rag. Twirls it taunt. Bends it in half. Dips the middle into wine. Sits calmly while the wine is absorbed. Removes. Wrings out excess.

Justin Maxwell

> *Puts the rag around his head like a bandage; the wine is blood over the ear. It stays there for the remainder of the play.*
>
> *He is then out of the ceremonial tone.*

When I gave me ear to my favorite whore, she was nonplussed. Called a doctor. Later, I apologized. She simply said that such things happen all the time in her world. She understands men who don't understand survival.

> ***VAN GOGH*** *spins the wheel.*

Exhausted Paint

Scene: Crows

*The bird has come up on the wheel. **VAN GOGH** goes to the wheel and removes it. This scene is whispered to the bird, a talismanic confidant.*

VAN GOGH
After I fail as a Parisian, and after I fail as an arts colony administrator slash roommate, and after I fail as a man with,
(He tries to look and see his own ear.)
well, let's call it stereophonic hearing,
I start to fail as a mental patient. This is when my success starts to take off.
(Makes a strange motion with the bird.)
Take a moment, think Van Gogh painting. That image in your head, I made it during this period.
I start to do . . . things, with colors and textures that art critics will fall in love with—after I die. If you go online to the Vincent Van Gogh museum's web page
(He stops. Realizing what he just said. Sits.)
The Vincent Van Gogh museum. Had you asked me in life and gotten an honest answer from me, I'd have told you it was a historical inevitability. The museum, not the web page. Or, I'd have told you it didn't matter a bit. Both are true.
(To crow.)
But you already know that.
(To audience.)
It's no secret that crows know secret things.
That's why they hoard and steal.
They're storing up spell components.
Their feathers are made of alchemy. Look closely at a crow. It's the color of transmogrification. It isn't really

Justin Maxwell

black. It's a past-blue. Or near-purple. It's a midnight vermillion. It's a secret color that only the crows have a name for.
I painted portraits more accurate than photographs.
I painted self-portraits with more shame and honesty than a confessional.
I painted landscape upon landscape—light and time.
I painted still-lifes that grow and move. I painted the incomprehensible finger print of God in each star.
I painted flowers that soften life and death.
I only painted crows once.
Even I have my limits. Some artists love crows like Mormons love seagulls. There's even a crow at the heart of the old Norse religion, so I know how dangerous they can be, in an ancestral way.
Sometimes, I suspect crows don't move.
Instead, they flap their wings and the universe moves around them. In my painting you can see the wheat field falling away from the crows.

> *The actor's attention focuses on the bird, not the audience. The crow becomes the center of the show, of our attention. It and **VAN GOGH** are in a private conversation.*

You did your terrible things in there. Your secret things. And I painted my secret paintings. I won't tell. I know you won't.
I don't know why you love me.
I don't know why you didn't stop it.
I could hear you deep inside the wheat when I started painting.
Could you hear my brushstrokes?
I could hear the measured, pearlescent blink of your

eyes. The inaudible slink-slink of your feathers preparing for flight.
Your cacophony of calls soaked me like the just-past rain.
Then the wheat fell away.
The reaper in his lavender shirt, from another day, saw his crop ascend like the damned. His ancestors in the dirt, the dirt in the wheat, the wheat in you. You in the sky. You absorbing all the light. The drinker-in of the world. Absorbing the seeds of my attention. Hovering on the canvass forever. For me. The peasant betrayed by God's grand design, again.
I just want to say thank you for keeping my secrets. I don't want to tell them everything.

> *He gives the crow an old kiss. And spins the wheel.*

Justin Maxwell

Scene: Fucking

The condom has come up on the wheel.

VAN GOGH

I could have used these—especially if the people who
claim I had syphilis were right.
I obsess about religion.
I obsess about money.
I obsess about success.
And, like one or two other artists you might know,
I obsess about women.
Especially the ones that are really bad for me.
Then I fall in love.
It starts innocently enough:
I perform the cultural equivalent of standing up at the
Thanksgiving dinner table and announcing to everyone
that I want to have sex with my hot cousin. But, I'm
Dutch, so I merely propose marriage to her.
For some reason she doesn't want me.
I blame her father,
and she turns to her fiancée for moral support.
I, of course, don't quit very easily.
To save you time:
I piss off everybody.
She avoids me for the rest of my life.
Her father threatens me.
My father considers trying to have me institutionalized,
again.
My brother gets on my case.
And he's paying the bills,
so he gets his way.
Eventually, my father and uncle grudgingly forgive me,
but they have to. They're Dutch.

Justin Maxwell

Then I fall in love.
With a pregnant woman.
Who is unmarried.
And a hooker.
I very much want to be a man of the people.
But her mom is a bitch.
Things go exactly how you'd expect.
I get her some medical care.
The kid comes along.
We're inseparable for about a year.
Everything goes to shit.
My brother gets on my case,
and he's paying the bills. . . .
Then I fall in love . . . .
    He spins the wheel.

Scene: Envelope

The envelope has come up on the wheel. ***VAN GOGH*** *takes it down and looks inside of it.*

VAN GOGH

My life is an envelope.
My brother Theo was my closest friend.
My brother Theo was my sole benefactor.
My brother Theo was my enemy.
> *(beat)*

My brother Theo saved all nine-hundred letters that I sent him. Of his letters to me only two or three survive; although, he clearly wrote more than I did. His librarian tendencies, after both our deaths, help establish me as a writer who was nearly as good as he was a painter.

(He holds open the envelope to the audience.)

Can you see all that in there?
His letters saved my life every week,
in every way you can think of.
An envelope is a surprising life raft.
The world shifts out from under us.
But an envelope?
Crisp, clean, square corners.
Life's safe when it has square corners.
And the origami of its folds provide
a kind of cosmic stillness.
> *(beat)*

All right. I know envelopes aren't origami; they're cut and glued. I know.
But I can imagine cosmic stillness.
I can imagine. Sometimes.
My life comes and goes in envelopes.
Checks from my brother,

my brother the art dealer.
When the lights are gone for the day
and the canvasses are stacked,
color becomes language, and I swirl myself into letters
that skitter off to my brother, my sister, and Gauguin,
Seurat, Pissaro,
and a Christie's auction worth of friends. All of whom
are in . . . need.
We love each other in our poor way.
We love our canvasses in our rich way.
We are loved.
But not in life so much.
Just in envelopes.

> *He spins the wheel.*

Exhausted Paint

Scene: Rebar

The iron bar has come up on the wheel. **VAN GOGH** *takes it and holds it in front of him like a prison bar; it holds the whole world of incarceration.*

VAN GOGH

I fail as a mental patient.
But I rather enjoy the experience.
The food isn't great, but it's free.
The room isn't great, but it's free.
Really, I'm better off in the asylum at Saint Remy
than at any other time in my life.
Bars don't block the wind.
Tendrils of breeze curl right around them.
The air is fresh.
I start painting roots,
twisting like serpents,
and my colors start to twist together,
and I get all wrapped up with . . . everything.
My belly is full of stars.
You can touch them if you want.
After the episode . . .
    (Waggles ear.)
I end up at the hospital at Arles.
then, later at the hospital at Avers-sur-Oise.
The . . . curator at the asylum is also an aspiring painter.
So once I get a little clear headed, he lets me paint on the grounds.
I make *Tree Roots and Trunks, Marguerite Gachet at the Paino*, and *Still Life: Vase with Flower and Thistle*.
I spend twenty-seven dollars and fifty-four cents on paint and canvas.

Justin Maxwell

I give one panting to the curator
and never sell the rest.
They're currently valued at sixty-seven-point-two, one hundred-eleven, and ninety-three million dollars respectively.
As I
    (Sarcastically.)
get better
they start to let me out of the asylum for painting excursions.
But when I get back,
my room is worse
the breeze is colder
the food is blander.
I want to move on; I make *Thatched Cottage by a Hill*, *Wheat Stacks with Reaper*, and the one you all know: *Wheat Field with Crows*.
And I spend thirty-two dollars even on paint and canvas.
Those three paintings are currently valued at ninety-two-point-four, one-hundred-one, and one hundred thirty-nine million respectively.
I lost three hundred thirty-two million, three hundred ninety-nine thousand, nine hundred, sixty-eight dollars on the exchange.
But it's art. So money doesn't matter.

    He spins the wheel.

Exhausted Paint

Scene: Light

The flashlight has come up on the wheel. **VAN GOGH** *removes it. He shines it on audience members, searching....*

VAN GOGH
(Lovingly.)
The light in my eyes in my self portrait,
is the light in your eyes of my painting.
Books and books and books have been written about light.
About the light in southern France.
About the light in my painting.
And light becomes its own tautology of painterly proof.
Hold me there. Inside you. Inside your eyes.
Inside your body.
Inside your head.
The light holds us together.

The light finds the woman it's looking for. **VAN GOGH** *goes to her.*

Just you and I, darling.
None of that collective, *audience*.
No forth wall.
Just us.
Just us and all this light.
It sheds out of the lights in the grid, and it scatters—diffuses, bounces off the floor, flickers off dust motes, off that lovely, threatening prop, objects scatter light everywhere while my voice directs your vision. But, now I want it here on me. The light bounces off me, rolls out from my costume, my hair, my sweat, my body. All

Justin Maxwell

of it light, rolling in bits, particle-waves breaking over your soft cornea and into the back of your eye, into your brain, your body, your corneal soul and the synaptic electricity of consciousness. This light is the titanium white on my canvasses. The color I ran out of most often. This is my gift to me of you; it is light off your face[1] into my eye. Carried in Shawn's memory. But it is this light roiling back and forth, living in a canvas that holds love. Our love. You. I. The dust motes. And all these shadowy witnesses. Please love me.

> ***VAN GOGH*** *turns the light out suddenly. He's out of the moment, drops his light, spins the wheel.*

---

[1] A word or two added to describe the audience member's face goes a long way here.

Exhausted Paint

Scene: Tree Root

The root has come up on the wheel. **VAN GOGH** *removes it. He tries to break it repeatedly during this scene, always failing.*

VAN GOGH
If you're not careful, a tree root can grow out of the ground, up around your aquifer ankle and draw you down,
into the earth.
It is very alarming to be under the earth.
There's very little light
and everything has a bluish tint,
like feldspar.
Both the mineral and the tree roots are faster than you think.
Or maybe I'm just too slow.
But all painters are slow men.
That's why so many of them work in studios.
The roots don't grow though the wooden floor.
The roots see the wooden floor, and they think: No, that's a friend of mine, better not. Or, they think: Shit! Look at what happened to that guy. And they stay away. Or, perhaps, they prefer to avoid cannibalism and don't eat their wooden brothers. I've no idea the thoughts of roots.
But they move with intention, and they move with randomness.
I hate the randomness and the intention. The intention of a world made by an all-knowing God is terrifying, embittering, and leaves me powerless to shape what I see. The randomness of roots, how they just lurk about in the darkness, spreading and growing into the unseen,

un-tasted damp. It smacks of malice. I understand roots like the veins and arteries of my own body. My own intention.
Roots can twist into any metaphor they want.

> ***VAN GOGH*** *stops trying to break the root. It begins its scary root dance.*

You might understand roots as a metaphor of:
>	the psyche
>	human history
>	depth
>	time
>	sturdiness
>	tradition
>	inbreeding
>	love
>	machinations.

All these are wrong.
Because I spend a lot of time outside, I've had the roots drag me down.
The roots mean whatever they want to mean,
and they do so
with mineral certainty.
I am a peasant at my canvases,
swinging away
at the mercy of grand forces
I can not stop or start of my own volition.
And the roots continue to grow.

> *The dance ends and* ***VAN GOGH*** *spins the wheel.*

Scene: Chairs

The tiny chair has come up on the wheel. He removes it and spends the scene trying to sit on it. This is heartbreaking, instead of slapstick.

VAN GOGH

It is good to build a room of blue,
and people it with wicker chairs.
The Bedroom is my best self-portrait;
it has no eyes.
The bedroom is inside the yellow house, now famous.
It has:
A warm bed, a green window, and two chairs.
Chairs are important:
God's sun burns down on us;
the sky lazes on forever;
the earth is eating upwards to reclaim her stolen nutrients;
but a good wicker chair will always come through for you.
Gauguin's chair was upholstered,
but he meant well.
My sister enjoyed overstuffed.
My brother liked solid wood.
My father preferred to stand.
I never had the heart to sit in Gauguin's chair.
I painted it in shadow.
Lit from behind, it is redbluegreen, against a chaotic carpet and two light sources—both burning. It's my only portrait of us.
Gertrude Stein will say that an artist always appears with their mouth firmly shut, and my self-portraits clearly show that I agree with her. But my chairs show

that I can scream too.
I wonder what kind of chairs Stein owned.

> ***VAN GOGH*** *abandons the chair like a question, and he spins the wheel.*

Scene: Cardboard Tube

The cardboard tube has come up on the wheel.

VAN GOGH
(Sincere, maybe a little desperate.)
Never keep a star inside your eye.
That's my advice to you.
I found Galileo's old telescope,
and I put it inside my brain.
It pulled the stars into my eyes.
I couldn't escape them.
Stars aren't pretty twinklings in the cool night sky.
Stars are roiling energy.
Stars are so big they move time around them.
The star in my eye spread through my body like a virus.
Like the syphilis that killed my brother.
It spread and it filled up my heart. Its energy coursing through my veins, radiating into canvas.
(Building mania.)
I painted two or three paintings a *day* with this solar infection. I painted a Louvre gallery in a month. In some weeks, I produced more masterpieces than most masters do in their careers.
(Down.)
I drank paint thinner.
It seemed like a good idea at the time.
I thought it might . . . clean the lens of the telescope, so to speak.
They put me on restriction at the asylum. I needed the rest. And the shade.
But it started out innocently enough. I was just a guy with a telescope in his brain, a young man in Paris, in the spring, and I wanted to paint a café. It's now called

Justin Maxwell

Café Van Gogh, by the way. I wanted normal things, you know, have a drink, impress a girl with some sketches. Maybe work on a pick up line: "Hey, baby, in 2007 they'll name this place after me." But instead, the nuclear chain reaction started. So I paint the café, and it's all . . . masterpiece. Then I go to put the stars in the sky. I mix, and dab a modicum of light onto the canvas. And it's wrong. And I think: How do you paint twinkling? Someday, I'll look at wheat and think: How do you paint heat? But my real thought will be: How do you paint twinkling? And the telescope will show me too much. And my blood will trundle through my body. And the stars will grow. And
(beat)
It just stops.
I painted stars.
My painting of humans at a café almost became a painting of stars.
I stopped it in the nick of time. But it would happen . . . .
(He sings from the Don McLean song.)
Starry, starry night.
Paint your palette blue and gray.
I freaking hate that Don McLean song.
Blue and gray—like I'm painting with the fucking Crayola eight box. Idiot.
Don't get me wrong. I love the attention.
But the song makes my work seem quaint. Like a print. Something you could hang on your bathroom wall to look at while you shit. Or, worse, to impress your guests.
I PAINTED THE SOULS OF STARS!
Stars are the engines God uses to make everything. Everything that isn't an atom of helium or an atom of hydrogen is the remnant of an exploded star. Really.
I tried to paint the whole void of the sky, on one clear

night.
And I failed.
The stars took over.
I wanted the void, the quiet,
with just one spire reaching up into the nothingness,
reaching for calm.
But the pulsing, plasma stars took over.
The stars knew my brain, knew what I could see.
And they showed me how to paint the spiraling cosmos,
about chaos, about wheels and the random order of
inevitable destruction.
That's what I saw with the telescope when I went
searching for calm.
At a certain point, the fire of liquor is soothing, the
ichor of tobacco is fluid, and turpentine is sweet.

> *He spins the wheel.*

Justin Maxwell

Scene: Iris

The iris has come up on the wheel.

VAN GOGH

I paint some irises, and my sister-in-law is amazed. She says that the eyes I paint hold the whole complexity of the human soul.
But she says it in French, so it's sexier.
I also paint flowers.
I hide people's souls in a little orb of color. Well, two orbs, so that you don't miss it. Frida Kahlo, God bless her, will need a whole canvass to paint her soul. I only need an orb. Need an iris. Need a palette of blue. And my paintings can go up in your living room, had any of you had the sense to buy when I was alive.
If she wasn't famous, how many of you would really hang a Kahlo in your living room? None. Exactly. But when I paint irises, it's a still life and a landscape at the same time. You can look at those flowers all day, because I've painted your own soul there. You may not know your soul is sweet blue, and brittle lavender, and sharp titanium, but that's okay. It is anyway. And if you live right, you've got a soft stem so blue it's green and so green it's blue.
I love you so much.
(beat)
Blue or green?
What color is my stem?
That's the question to guide you through life!
And look for the painterly answer.
Think about motion, and about shape;
think of colors next to one another; remember color is a neighborly thing.

Justin Maxwell

Never answer: Beige.
Beige is the color of suicide. No one has ever committed suicide in a green room.
Yes, I know: Vinnie, you *shoot yourself* outside. And *outside* is just chock full of green.
But in my defense, it was a particularly beige day. Plus, a dirt road, a parched wheat field rolling up a hillside, and a sky of Bethlehem brown that calls you up to the bottom of God's filthy foot. And in a beige box like that, all you can do is shoot yourself and die in your brother's arms. It was a bonding experience for us, our two green stems alone in a vase with a lovely room around us. A few fallen petals on the table top. And me moaning in agony for a few days while I slowly died of pain. It was like Mantegna's *St. Sebastian* with all those arrows, but less phallic. And done by me instead. It was like how your back would feel if you stood motionless on a gallery floor for three days looking at Mantegna's painting. Terribly painful. Terribly boring. But less phallic.
A patch of irises can hold your soul; look in your mirror after the show. Look closely. And if that doesn't work for you. Try it at night with a blue eyed girl. You'll see it's true.

> *He gives the flower to an audience member and spins the wheel.*

Exhausted Paint

Scene: Nephew

*The sheaf of paper/notebook comes up on the wheel. Throughout this scene **VAN GOGH** does not actually write on the pages, or make a pretense of doing so. He directly addresses the audience.*

VAN GOGH

Thirty-one January, eighteen-ninety.
To my dear nephew,
I write this letter to you, on the day of your birth, to welcome you into the world with a heart full of love.
(He tears out the page. Crumples it up. Throws it into the audience.)
Bull shit.
Thirty-one January, eighteen-ninety.
Bon soi, my lovely nephew,
Your parents have named you after me and I am writing to greet you at the start of a good life of warm winters, and cool summers, and a lush palette.
(He tears out the page. Crumples it up. Throws it into the audience.)
Fuck no. Lush palette. Goddamn.
Thirty January, eighteen-ninety.
Tomorrow you shall be born, my Vincent.
Dear God! What a day it shall be.
Dear God. Say it like a prayer.
Dear God. Say it like a curse.
For you, my new nephew. First. Last. Only. Nephew.
For you, blessed namesake. Cursed namesake. I make a present. A new noun: Happy-sad. Connected with a hyphen. A compound noun. Two words become one. Your parents come together. You and world connected. I

and my loneliness, connected. You and I. The world will make you happy. The world will make you sad. It will be wonderful. It will be terrible. You will never know me. You will carry me forward into every introduction. You and your mother will carry on my brother's great work—caring for me. Carrying my work into the world, into the future. I will be warmly in the happy-sad dirt, friends with the maggots that eat my eyes.

> *(He tears out the page. Crumples it up. Throws it into the audience.)*

Thirty-two January, eighteen-ninety.

> *(whispering)*

Welcome to our secret day. This is the lonely-love day. Another hyphen for our secret, new world. Don't tell your father. This day is a holiday—a break away from the ones forced to show up on the calendar. A day so all alone even the other days don't know about it. Really. Ask December 6th, ask May 1st, ask September 11th, ask December 25th, ask July 4th. None of them know about this day, all by itself, off playing in a meadow. It is the best day. All your loves are on this day. All the births. All the fortune. This is the day the tobacco is moist and the water is crisp. It's like your favorite brothel, right after bath day.

And I'm sharing it with you because . . .

> *He very suddenly crumples up the paper. Then un-crumples and tears it into confetti very quickly. Then he picks up the scraps and puts them in his pocket.*

Thirty-one January, eighteen-ninety.
To my nephew.
Dear sir. I am afraid to say, you are fucked. Just by being

Exhausted Paint

born. Too late for you dude. And too late for me. My brother loves me more. Buys my paint, pays my bills. Loves me. And he loves you too. But how much love will be left over for you? You will be alone. Like me. You will be poor like me. You will be unloved . . . also like me.

>*(He tears out the page. Crumples it up. Throws it into the audience.)*

Thirty-one January, eighteen-ninety.
To my Dear Nephew.
I write this letter to you, on the day of your birth, to welcome you into the world with a heart full of love.
Etcetera, etcetera, etcetera.
You uncle,
Vincent.

>*He spins the wheel.*

Justin Maxwell

Scene: Diamonds

The lump of coal has come up on the wheel. ***VAN GOGH*** *puts on gloves and removes it. Over the course of the next scene he will slowly crumple it apart in his hands, as though he's searching for something.*

VAN GOGH

Diamonds reveal the kaleidoscopic heart of light.
They are perfect, as far as I know.
Diamonds are an allotrope of carbon,
made up of a rigid lattice formed from covalent tetrahedral bonding. I know because I'm a painter, and we painters know such things.
History books will never tell you the first diamond was discovered in India on December 28th, two thousand seven hundred eighteen, BCE, along the South bank of the Godavari River. The discoverer had no idea that the next closest thing to diamond is graphite, which is used to cool and control the thermonuclear reactions in power plants, and in pencils. But they knew the find was important. Diamonds quickly became objects of great value—had they known what British colonialism would do to them, I suspect they'd have put the diamonds back. Look at what diamonds have done to Angola, Sierra Leone. Look at what the diamonds have done to Amsterdam. Look at what light has done to me.
I learned to disassemble diamonds.
Not cut them. Not cleave. But disassemble.
That's valuable because inside of a diamond is light.
Perfect light.
Mutable, shifting light.
Light one can lay in a painting.

Justin Maxwell

Light one can excite their paint with.
Light I can make waltz on a canvas.
It is perfect.
And perfection is important.
It is also obtainable.
You just have to work harder.
I just have to work harder.
Each painting is perfect because I make the light move.
And light is perfect. And I put it in my paint, like God put it in the world.
I get a little carried away sometimes.
But if you're going to take on the pressure of being an artist,
you should know its going to crush you down into diamond.

> ***VAN GOGH*** *shows the coal in his hands as though he's going to reveal a gem, but no gem. Just coal. He takes off the gloves and spins the wheel.*

Scene: Conclusion

The wheel is empty. ***VAN GOGH*** *picks up the black square and re-attaches it to the wheel, front and center.*

VAN GOGH
At the end, I am crushed by light. Exhausted.
Between this stage
and the colorless void of space
there is a kaleidoscope of atmospheres that translates
light into something usable.
Because we've evolved to live in the atmosphere, we forget that it is crushing, and we call it one atmosphere of pressure.
The light sinks down on us, and we are at the bottom of a great ocean of visible light.
Between this stage and the void is fifty-four thousand five hundred sixty fathoms of atmosphere.
I paint outside.
I carry all that weight right, balanced, on the crown of my head.
I first noticed it at the asylum, which had a thick stone roof, and small windows. Little light got in. The asylum held up the unfathomable atmosphere, so I could get better, go outside. Paint. Collapse back to the asylum. Outside. Paint. Collapse. Asylum again. Nephew gets born. Paint. Collapse. New Asylum. You get the timeline. The facts don't matter, and at the end, they mean even less than ever before. One day, I decide to drink turpentine again. So clear. So sweet that it can wipe away all the colors. All of them. But I was out of turpentine that day.
So I shot myself.

Justin Maxwell

I wanted to let the light trickle in.
To rivulet in.
To stream in.
To flow.
To spray.
To glug.
To fill up the ship.
It takes a long time for the thick paint to dry,
to exhaust its camphors and its spirits.
You can see them departing the body of the composition,
if you look closely enough.
I have failed.
I reached for the brass ring.
And I missed.
And I learned what happens when someone like me misses.
We reach again.
And then we miss.
We reach again.
The cycle repeats itself.
Some of my peers catch the ring.
I do not.
The spirits leave the paint dry,
denuded and ready for the ages,
for art critics, curators, collectors,
all of you,
the merchandise buying public.
I am well-remembered.
I would have rather been well-known.
I needed to show you the illusion,
Show you how the paint is not the painting.
All the symptoms that I display
that history uses to explore the

whoever-I-was
are all symptoms of *pressure*.
We reach for the ring,
reach again.
On July 27th, in the open air, near Auvers-sur-Oise,
France, I go out for a day of frantic reaching.
And on that day . . .
BAM!
I crushed me.
    (To audience member.)
Give me my gun back.

        Dark. End of play.

Justin Maxwell

Acknowledgments

The list of people to whom I owe a thank you is very long. With the myriad performances, readings, and discussions that prefigure a collection of short plays, keeping track of everyone who influenced a script far surpasses my librarian tendencies. The list of people to whom I owe far more than a thank you approaches the mind-boggling. In looking at the list, I wonder how someone so reclusive can have so many friends, loved ones, and supporters. In that wondering, I become profoundly grateful for all of you who are so dedicated to my work. I'm a little overwhelmed by the number of people who follow-up a standard greeting by asking when they can see the next play. I am so grateful for the friends and family members who offered physical and emotional support while I've walked to the back of so many dead ends and turned around again. To the actors, dramaturges, directors, and producers that have worked at tables, and in conference rooms, and on stages listening to the difficult early drafts of these little plays: Thank you all.

I need to thank Susan Maxwell and Maryann Fenz because I couldn't have done any of this without their lifelong support; the Johnson/Hanson family for their faith in me; Josh, Lukas, and Zak Maxwell for always reminding me that a certain weirdness runs in the family; and the McGrath and Reinbird clans for always celebrating the weirdness.

I need to thank Chuck Radder for all the tolerance and friendship. Matt Osterhaus too. Toby Thelin and Patrice Miller who have invested so much time in keeping my words in the mouths of actors. To The Brick theatre in Williamsburg for being so open to outsiders and the unexpected. To 'Pataphysics workshops and Mac Wellman for encouraging innovation.

I need to thank The Playwrights' Center in Minneapolis, along with Polly Carl, Christina Ham, and Rachel Greene for their support. To Greg Giles who saw that I was

Justin Maxwell

a playwright back in grad school, before I saw it. To Hamline University's MFA for being a place where a poet could become a playwright: Mary Rockcastle, Patricia Francisco, Larry Suttin, Jim Moore, and Roseann Lloyd. To Danette Olsen, Ed Moersfelder, and the folks at Festival Theatre for being so joyful. To Shawn Boyd whose enthusiasm for my work led directly to Exhausted Paint and is the trailhead leading into this collection. To Christopher Kidder-Mostrom and Commedia Beauregard who are directly responsible for some of the material in the collection. To Swandive Theatre, Meaghan DiSciorio, Damon Runnals, and Bryan Grosso, who just keep encouraging me!

I need to thank my friends and colleagues at the Mid-American Theatre Conference whose fingerprints are on many pages of this collection: Milbre Birch, Vanessa Marie Campagna, Season Ellison, Kristi Good, Shawna Mefferd Kelty, Wes Pearce, Jane Purse-Wiedenhoeft, Tom Robson, Bryan Vandevender, and Ron Zank.

Made in the USA
Columbia, SC
11 December 2024